The
VALUE
Economy

*Thriving Together at
the End of
the World of Work*

The VALUE Economy

Thriving Together at the End of the World of Work

HEATHER McCONNELL

The Value Economy: Thriving Together at the End of the World of Work

ISBN-13: 978-1533363725
ISBN-10: 1533363722

Cover and interior art: Diane A. Curran, *www.TheMarketingDeal.com*
Cover design: Jamie Warren, Loose Change Studio
Interior design: Carol Russo, Carol Russo Design
E-book edition published September 2016
Print edition published September 2016

This paperback edition was printed by Createspace.

TheValueEconomy.com

Contents

To the Dancers and Dreamers, Poets and Painters, Musicians and Magicians, Singers and Sewers, Weavers and Wanderers, Carvers and Cooks, Writers and Rhymers, Explorers and Engineers, Bakers and Binders, Teachers and Students, Welders and Healers, Designers and Shapers, Coders and Crafters, Potters and Planters, Physicians and Physicists, Playwrights and Sculptors, Architects and Archaeologists, Speakers and Readers, Runners and Swimmers, Protectors and Fighters, Cutters and Fitters, Mosaicists and Makers, Sowers and Seers, Editors and Inventors . . .

To all of us in our continuous, creative, passionate, valuable searching.

The End of Work as We Know It

All around us, we hear stories about how workers are losing their jobs. Some of them may be friends and family, some we see on the news or hear about through social media, or you may even be one of the millions of people who have lost their livelihood in the last few years.

Even finding work can be nearly impossible and people are going to extraordinary lengths in search of employment, traveling huge distances across national borders and sometimes even through warzones.

We also hear, especially in this American election year, lots of talk about fixing the problem, that politicians are going to bring back the old jobs, create masses of new ones or that the unemployment rate is really going down, there are more jobs than we think, and it's really all okay.

But we don't really believe the politicians or the feel-good stories and we are worried. We sense that there is something very wrong, not just here in the U.S. but globally.

We're right to worry.

Two massive socio-economic disruptions are crashing together across our planet: technological automation eliminating millions of jobs and a growing, cheap labor pool due to immigration, globalization, and our longer lifespans competing for what's left.

The old jobs are disappearing forever. There's nothing we can do about that. But there is path through the coming storm.

What Robots Can't Do

The scientific and technological breakthroughs of the Industrial Revolution did a terrific job of raising living standards for people all over the world. Millions of farmers, ranchers, and other agrarian workers migrated into cities which then turned into the megalopolises we have today.

But the Industrial Revolution also automated *people*. For the first time in human history, we worked by the clock, often doing the exact same task over and over for days, weeks, even years on end. Human beings became just another component of the giant mechanical devices that produced the mass-made goods needed to support the growing population.

The more recent Tech Revolution has gifted us with far less physical labor - we now sit at desks most of the day which presents a different sort of problem—but the idea of humans as machine components has not changed much.

Very soon, far more sophisticated machines driven by artificial intelligence will be here though and exactly *because* they are machines they will be better at doing mechanical work than we are. As these machines become smarter, they will eliminate many jobs that we thought were irreplaceable just a few years ago. White collar jobs which have any degree of repetitive work such as bank services, office administration, and customer service are already disappearing.

But there are some things robots will never be able to do and one of these is the human ability to feel passionate about our work. Whether you're an archaeologist unearthing ancient cities, a scientist tracking down the cure to a deadly virus, or a musician creating new kinds of music by mashing together traditional sounds, robots simply don't and never will have the passion that you can bring. A robot can be a helpful tool for an archaeologist, a researcher or a musician but it can't be inspired by other humans or their stories.

This is precisely because robots *are* machines. Robots can't do the work that humans do with such heart and soul because robots do not have hearts and souls. We do.

The Value Economy

What are you passionate about? What do you care the most about? If you're in love with your job, that's great! But for many of us what feeds our souls is found elsewhere. Hobbies, crafts, social clubs, sports, games, there are as many unique activities that make our hearts sing as there are people on the planet.

And we accomplish these labors of love passionately and unstoppably not for any compensation but because they fulfill our lives.

These things we do with our hearts and souls, out of love for art, science, or humanity, or just plain old curiosity, with totally committed bodies and minds, are where the Value Economy truly lies.

And this is how we will find our way through the old

machine-driven system, to a new creative, passionate economy by Valuing Ourselves, Valuing Each Other, and Valuing Our World.

VALUING OURSELVES

Acknowledge

One of the toughest things you can ask someone to do is something we should all be good at. But most of us are terrible at it.

Truly accepting acknowledgment is extremely difficult for most people. If you ask someone to get up in front of a large crowd of people and graciously accept their acknowledgment that individual will almost always say something like, "Aw, shucks. It was nothing."

Getting someone to just stand for a moment and accept praise is very hard to do.

Why?

There are probably millions of theories out there but I think there's a sneaky one underneath it all.

If we don't allow other people to acknowledge our own greatness then we don't have to either and we can continue living our lives in the belief that we aren't capable of more.

The truth is that we are capable of a lot more.

The most important part of building a Value Economy starts with the individual. You have to truly acknowledge yourself and your potential. Not that you're going to be Superman or Wonder Woman tomorrow morning but that you really are capable of a whole lot.

This isn't easy. (There's also a lot of false bravado around. Don't go that way.)

Take a moment every so often to look back on your life and acknowledge that you've accomplished quite a bit. Make a list. One great way to see how much you've done is by updating your resume (even if you're not in search of a new job). Do it with the mindset of being up on that stage. Ask others what skills and talents they see in you that you might be missing. Pay extra attention to those areas where you describe your hobbies and interests. Sometimes there are talents hiding there you might not have thought of as especially important before but that could be valuable in today's more creative jobs market.

And now more than ever, please realize that you are being bombarded constantly with media that is telling you that you are Not Good Enough and Never Will Be. They are wrong.

(But they're making tons of money off our fear so they're not going to stop doing it anytime soon.)

So acknowledge yourself. And if you happen to be up on that stage, take it in. Acknowledge the acknowledgers. They believe in you and you need to believe in yourself *and* their belief in you.

Fair Pay

Have you ever asked for a raise? (Or, if you are self-employed, given yourself one?) If so, congratulations. It's probably the easiest way to increase your income but many people never even ask.

We seem to go through life receiving the pay that we do because we are satisfied with that amount though we really aren't happy at all. But we don't ask for more money either because we believe our bosses are already paying us what they can afford, or because we are afraid of losing our jobs.

Asking for a raise (and negotiating in general) isn't taught in schools and often not at home and so we continue, underpaid and scrimping, when the only thing standing between us and more money is a conversation.

This fact clearly shows us the value we assign ourselves.

Women who are often brought up to be non-confrontational are particularly poor (literally) at asking for a raise.

But we need to. We all need to. In fact, we need to demand a living wage, not just for ourselves, but because no one should be working as hard as they can for 40+ hours a week and not be compensated with enough to buy food, pay for housing, take care of their kids, and pay their bills.

This used to be the American dream. Get a job and a decent salary with a raise every year. No more.

We need to fix this.

Why? Why shouldn't we accept—as so many financial analysts tell us—what the market will bear?

Well, for one very good reason: right now some American businesses are underpaying the workforce so much that those underpaid workers are no longer spending their wages on American goods. And that's hurting our economy. And because our economy is closely tied into the global economy, it's also hurting other countries.

Empowering American workers doesn't just help us, it helps the world.

Artists are the Worst

When I say artists, I mean creative people of all kinds. Poets, writers, potters, sculptors, painters, musicians, singers, dancers, almost anyone consumed by a creative endeavor.

I suspect that one reason they are so bad at asking for money is that they're busy doing their art and having fun. But I don't know for sure. I do know that they:

1. Give a lot of their work away for free (Sometimes this is for 'exposure' but as one creative type I know put it, "I'm dying of 'exposure'!");
2. Give a lot of their work to their friends and charities for nothing; and
3. When they do ask for money, don't ask for enough.

So, if you are a creative type, please take a good look at what you are charging and whether it's enough. A very dear artist friend (who is also partly responsible for inspiring this book) finally raised his rates a few years ago. He was pleasantly surprised to find that:

1. Clients paid more promptly;
2. Better-paying clients appeared; and
3. He had more time to work on his art!

Educate

With all the doom and gloom of today's news headlines, you may not have noticed that stories of education success have been popping up like never before. Whether it's a new school in rural Africa, street kids in New Delhi teaching themselves how to use a computer[1], or droves of children (and adults) enrolling in online courses, we are all learning things at an extraordinary rate.

Many people are going back to school to get that added edge for the current job market. The more we learn, the more possibilities we create for our future. But many of us are also just curious. We want to learn more not just for our careers but because we just want to know and understand.

And we're curious about everything. Astronomy, ancient history, technology, advances in medicine. Just take a look at the latest offerings on TED.com and you'll be amazed (as well as distracted for the next several hours. . . .)

All of this push towards increasing education is important for far more than satisfying our curiosity.

Why? Because we're going to need all hands on deck for the global challenges we'll face in this century and beyond.

We need more teachers teaching all ages and abilities, we need more scientists researching climate change, cures for diseases, and ways to feed a growing population with quality nutrition, and we need more engineers to build cities in new ways we can't yet imagine. And we need more astronauts. Really. We're going to go to Mars in the next few decades. And back to the Moon. And probably a whole lot of other places. We're going to go because we can and we're curious creatures, and we've never been able to resist exploring new frontiers. And we're going to learn even more things we can't begin to imagine when we do.

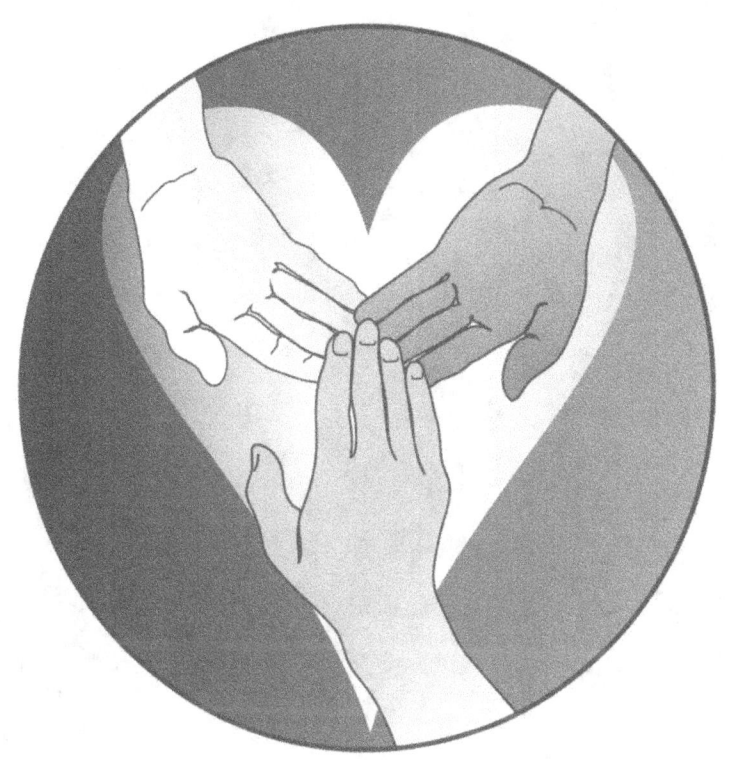

VALUING EACH OTHER

Encourage

The word "encourage" tells you everything you need to know about it if you look at its roots. It simply means to "make or put in" "heart or courage," literally to "hearten" or "make strong."

We need courage. The news media is telling us about once an hour that the world is ending, and though their hysterical pronouncements have not yet come true, we do face a lot of challenges.

We don't have much control over most of it. But we can make little changes, random acts of kindness, keeping in touch with old and new friends, donating some small change to whatever charity is asking for it at your local grocery store.

It adds up.

Just really "being" with your family and friends is an

important way to add encouragement. Put the cell phone in airplane mode or turn it off entirely and listen, really listen to what they have to say. You don't need to fix any problems they might tell you about. Just listen. That's enough.

People want to matter, they want to do things that make a difference in the world. They want to be able to take pride in their work and have it mean something. Respect this. Their path may be completely different than yours but they are doing the best they can. Encourage them.

Calling Miss America

A long time ago, I would wake up at 5 a.m. to catch an early bus for my 9-5 job in Midtown Manhattan. Along with thousands of other sleepy and weary women, I would shuffle into the hustle and bustle of Port Authority an hour and half later. I was barely awake and I did not feel pretty.

But an old homeless man always sat on the lowest step of one of the unused stairwells and as we all trudged by he would call out, "Here she comes, Miss America! Oh, Miss America! Lookin' great today!" I would always find myself smiling a tiny bit and my step would lighten just a little. I'm sure it brought a few more coins to his cup but he also seemed to genuinely enjoy cheering all of us up in those grueling hours. Kindness does not depend on income.

Pay Fairly

We live in a culture where we are constantly scrambling for the lowest price on everything we could possibly want or need.

Our capitalist society has been infected with the belief that we should spend a significant part of our lives scoping out the best deals for everything, clipping coupons, bargaining down every price possible, and buying goods that because they are cheaply made fall apart quickly. Then we throw the stuff out and replace it with newer junk. Our landfills are full of never worn clothes, barely used household items, and food that spoiled because we bought too much or just didn't eat it in time.

We don't need this stuff. And we also don't need to spend so much of our hard-earned cash on it.

Instead, we could buy slightly more expensive but better quality goods that last ten times as long. We could buy less but better quality food (which might also help our waistlines).

This discounted race to the bottom shows up everywhere: in the loss of high-quality American manufacturing; airline seats that require pain meds to tolerate; and cheap junk food that is killing us among many other examples.

For a little more money, time, and effort, we could enjoy unique handcrafted furnishings in our homes, air travel that might even be enjoyable, and fantastic local cuisines.

But instead, we insist on getting the best deal. Is it worth it? We need to start asking that question.

Even more important than the money we don't spend on goods is the money we don't spend on services.

Low wages are becoming alarmingly low—unpaid internships seem to have become the norm and brand-new graduates are facing unprecedented wage stagnation[2].

This just doesn't make sense. We can do much better for our young people entering into the job market. And given the levels of youth unemployment across the world, it's not just in America that we need to start paying people and paying them fairly.

An old writer friend of mine used to spend a considerable amount of time in diners and coffee shops scribbling away.

He always tipped generously and as a result his coffee cup was always full, frequently with freshly-made ground roast. Even if you can't pay much, it pays to pay fairly.

Share

There's a lot of talk these days about the "sharing economy" where people share things they own with others in return for some profit. The best known examples are Airbnb which allows homeowners to rent out part or even all of their home for short periods of time and Uber which matches up people needing a ride somewhere with those who have cars and some spare time. New "sharing" websites seem to appear online daily—you can even rent clothing, purses, and power tools.

All of these new services connecting people in novel ways are dependent on the internet but I think they're actually based on a much older system of trade.

They're a modern recreation of the old barter systems except that now you can exchange things and services with people on the other side of the planet.

The non-traditional marketplace for goods and services has suddenly gotten huge.

This also poses some dangers because it could drastically undercut market prices.

But the Sharing Economy is not going away anytime soon.

And it can help save a lot of people a lot of money. Plus it helps put money in the hands of individuals and small businesses.

But one of the best and unexpected side effects of this new style of doing business is that we are also sharing ourselves.

People are connecting to do business and in the process, establishing personal relationships with complete strangers. And these relationships are resulting not just in mutually beneficial sharing agreements but in more connection throughout our communities and even more creative sharing.

So, in what ways can you be a part of your community and share yourself?

If you own a business, what about sharing that knowledge with someone who's just starting up in exchange for a small discount?

If you love to sew and make things, what about showing a teenager who's interested how to repair and make their own clothes in exchange for some help with yard work?

Or, if you're a writer looking for story ideas, what about sitting with some of the older people in your community to listen to them?

The Sharing Economy is changing our economic system dramatically but even more amazing is how people are creatively sharing themselves as never before. This is far more important than the money we save and earn. We are creating communities out of nothing and that is where the real magic is.

VALUING COMMUNITY

Participate

As we move further into the 21st century, you might think we would be happier with all the benefits that modern technology has brought us. But this isn't true. The starkest demonstration of this fact is the increasing rate of suicide in America. You may have heard about the numbers of veterans taking their own lives but did you also know that the overall age-adjusted suicide rate for those under 75 in the U.S. was 24% higher in 2014 than in 1999[3]?

There are many reasons for this tragic increase including the current opioid epidemic and declining economic opportunities but loss of community also plays a significant role.

We used to be a country of small towns. We're now a country filled with isolated individuals in cities and sprawling suburbs who are posting on social media about TV shows they are more familiar with than their own neighborhoods.

What can be done about this isolationism? Build community.

Join local organizations. Talk to your neighbors. Host a dinner party. Join a hiking club. Help clean-up an empty lot and then turn it into a sports field for the neighborhood kids. There are billions of ways to connect with other people.

It's not like we don't have the time—we're watching nearly three hours of TV a day.[4]

Besides connecting with people in your community, you can also help those who might need a little more by creating a social enterprise.

With a social enterprise, you create a socially oriented business where any profits made are put back into the employees and the business rather than the owners of the company. Maximizing social impact (addressing issues such as homelessness, the environment, and education for examples) is the target rather than pleasing shareholders.

One example of a social enterprise might be teaching unemployed military veterans how to make furniture which can then be sold. The profit can be used to buy more raw materials and tools, and to support further teaching. One group I came across would work to build up enough to buy a whole workshop for a disabled veteran then that veteran would work with others to save up for another workshop. And the vets gained skills as they learned that they could then use to find jobs or continue on teaching other vets.

What needs does your community have that a social enterprise might meet?

Invest Local

In April 2016, the "Panama Papers" story broke and the world learned about trillions of dollars concealed in offshore tax havens by thousands of people all across the globe. Wealthy people from countries both rich and poor were taking money out of the communities they lived in and instead hiding the loot away where no one had access to it.

What if they had instead chosen to invest even a small portion of that money back into their communities? What if they had funded a few small business start-ups by young entrepreneurs?

Can you imagine the benefits of such an investment?

We might have cured cancer by now. At the very least, there might be fewer hungry children on the planet.

Money doesn't do much when it just sits still. But when it gets moving, wow, can it change things.

So, if you are fortunate enough to have some extra cash, consider investing it back into your community. Find a local entrepreneur who wants to start a business and help them out. (If you've got experience running a business, they might also appreciate some tips.)

A great way to discover people in your community to invest in is to join the local Chamber of Commerce and other business-oriented local organizations.

People across the world are moving to urban areas and a lot of rural small villages and towns are disappearing. What isn't going away is the need for communities and connection. So, whether you're living in an urban high rise in Hong Kong, on the outskirts of a thriving new African city, or in a historic Washington, D.C suburb, there are people organizing and working together to help each other. Invest in those people.

You might be surprised at the results.

Invest Global

Paradoxically, one way to build local community is to reach out globally. You might be surprised at how easy this is. There are probably connections to people in every corner of the world right in your own hometown. All you have to do is start talking and you'll find out that the daughter of a friend from high school went into the Peace Corps and met the love of her life in Macedonia. Or maybe you've met people in your church choir who happen to collect African art and know a few artists in Uganda. Or... well, you get the picture. It's pretty easy (and fun!) to find those connections. Then, someone might come up with a fundraiser idea, say a concert by some of your musician friends because maybe that Ugandan artist knows of an orphanage that could use some help. And suddenly you're talking on Skype with people in a rural African village.

Besides building community, you might also find there are

positive economic side-effects to this kind of global connecting. Maybe some of the women in east Africa you've connected with are making extraordinary hand-crafted cloth that is just perfect for light-as-air summer clothing in the hot sun of the deserts of southern California. Or someone in south India has developed the perfect spices for a fish curry to liven up your New England restaurant's menu.

As technology and other forces keep displacing workers in old industries, we must keep striving to carve out new markets for our quality creative goods and services. These markets not only can but absolutely will be global. There are local musicians all over the world for instance—heavy metal bands in Iran, Mongolian rappers, and classical music orchestras in the slums of South America—who have found devout audiences in every corner of the globe.

These are the creative connections we need to keep building to get through the economic storms of the coming years. We need to let go of the idea that any big company will be around long enough to provide us with decent wages for our entire lives. Or that our governments can. Only we can make our own paths through the coming economic storms by valuing ourselves, valuing each other, and valuing our communities to build the creative and passion-driven connected world we all want to live in.

Why a Value Economy
Is Inevitable

Think about the future for a moment. Now think about the far future. What do you see? Whatever you imagine is probably not what the present looks like. We know there are going to be changes. Big changes. We know because we have seen it in our own lifetimes. Not just the ever-increasing sophistication of our phones and computers and other gadgets. But because we've nearly eradicated polio. And because we've been to the moon. And because we're living longer than our ancestors.

We know things are changing.

Just over ten years ago, no one knew what a smart phone was. Think about that. Just ten years.

So what's going to happen in the next ten years that we don't know about and can't imagine? The next one hundred?

There are a lot of "post-apocalyptic" science fiction movies and there's good reason to worry with everything we see on the news.

But there's one thing that a lot of these movies don't take into account.

That's the human capacity for caring.

We haven't exploded a nuclear bomb as a weapon of war since 1945.

Disaster relief agencies and governments have saved millions of lives just because human beings in different countries have reached out and given generously sometimes even in the face of wars between their own countries.

Millions of people volunteer every year for thousands of non-profits with the only goal of helping those in need.

Yes, there have been terrible atrocities but there also have been incredible acts of humanity.

The number of children under five dying from hunger-related causes has been halved in just the last twenty-five years and that's with the increase in population[5]. More kids, especially girls, are in school than ever before[6]. People are living longer, and yes, the world is even becoming less violent[7]. (Despite the news reports to the contrary, fewer people are dying in armed conflict than ever before.) And although income inequality is way too high, people all over the planet are, quite loudly, expressing their outrage over this and the corruption too often behind it. That, in itself, is a positive sign.

Creating a Value Economy is about believing in the good in other human beings. About having faith in each other. Not without reason but because, deep down, we all want a better world where all human beings have the opportunity to fully express themselves. Choose to believe in this. Then it will happen. It's inevitable.

Building Blocks for a Value Economy

The Value Economy encompasses three principles: Valuing Ourselves, Valuing Each Other, and Valuing Our Communities. That's it. This book doesn't have all the answers—it's a starting point. Because there are as many ways to create a Value Economy as there are human beings on the planet. Following are some of the specific ideas mentioned in the previous pages plus a few more. I've also left lots of blank space for you to add your own thoughts and ideas.

Valuing Ourselves: Acknowledge

➤ Accept acknowledgement. This may actually be harder than you think but keep practicing. And remember to acknowledge those who are acknowledging you.

➤ Acknowledge your body. Exercise. This is great for getting and keeping in shape. (It is also great for lowering healthcare costs.) A lot of us don't like to exercise or feel that we don't have enough time for it. But there are many ways to do just a little exercise (including a lot of smartphone apps) and lots of people who can help you. There are way too many underemployed physical trainers in the world right now. Take care of your body and remember that this can also be fun. If you don't like one type of exercise, keep experimenting until you find something you do. Today, you can find classes for every kind of workout imaginable and many you've probably never even heard of. (Who had heard of Zumba just a few years ago?)

➢ If you are sick, rest. Too many people are working when they shouldn't be. Take your sick days and avoid infecting your fellow employees. And ask for help if you need it.

➢ Take care of your body and the planet. Eat less. Since we have reached a (literal) tipping point on the planet where there are more overweight people than those who are not getting enough nutrition, I am guessing that you might be on a diet. I know I am. Besides the healthy aspects of a lower weight, there is the obvious correlation that you eat less food and create a smaller carbon footprint on the planet.

➢ Take a good look at how you dress, your posture, the way you present yourself. Are you truly showing the world who you really are and can be? Or are you hiding something? It's extremely hard to honestly and fairly appraise yourself—to see your beauty as well as all the negatives we focus on—as hard as being up on that stage accepting acknowledgement! But to truly value yourself, you need to share your own inner beauty with others.

➢ Take care of your heart and soul. It's hard to remember to do this in all the hustle and bustle of our daily lives but make a little time (even 5 minutes) for yourself each day to meditate. (Sleeping doesn't count!)

➢ Carve out time for creative pursuits. Though it may seem

like you're putting in energy you don't have, you'll actually find you have more energy to do the things you need to if you squeeze in a little time now and then to feed your soul.

➤ Redo your resume (even if you're not looking for a job). And ask for others' input. You may be surprised at the talents others see in you that you can't see.

Valuing Ourselves: Fair Pay

➤ Ask for a raise. If you're nervous or have other reservations, think of it this way: you're not asking just for yourself, you're asking for all the people you will be turning that money over to. You're part of the economy and your money helps to support others, from the farmers who produce the groceries at your local store to the teachers who are paid through your taxes to the up-and-coming young musicians playing their first gig at your favorite restaurant.

➤ If you are not being paid fairly in your job, communicate this to your employer. Do your research on what you feel would be fair and why, and then present this information to your employer. If your employer responds positively, then great. However, if they don't, then you are not being acknowledged at the level you need to be.

➤ If you are not being paid fairly and not being acknowledged in your workplace, start looking for another job. Too many people feel that they can't leave their jobs when, in reality, they are simply succumbing to fear. Getting past that fear and realizing your true potential isn't easy but it is worth it. We all have a limited number of years on this planet—why spend them doing work that doesn't stretch you to your full potential? Why play small?

➤ If you are looking for work, there are hundreds of websites willing to help you. If you find yourself full of fear about the possibility of leaving your old job for a new one, just spend some time looking through these websites. They are full of tips and encouragement to help you make the best break possible.

➤ If you are a starving actor, artist, writer, musician, etc.., look for grants, scholarships, loans, anything you can find to support yourself and your dreams. This is another way to take money from large corporations and the 1% and redistributing it to the bottom of the food chain, i.e. you. (Sorry but it's true.) And keep working on your craft and putting it out there. We can never have enough beautiful art of all kinds in the world.

➤ If you can't find work no matter how hard you try, keep trying. Keep reworking that resume, learning new skills, and honing old ones. This isn't important just for you. It's important because you are a unique individual with talents and gifts only you can give to the world. Sometimes it takes a while to figure out what those are but if you persist, sooner or later you will. (Some people will then say that you are an "overnight success"! As a friend once remarked to me, "Yes, a 20-year overnight success!")

➤ When you do have money to spend, spend wisely. Buy clothing that will last. Better yet, hire a seamstress to help you repurpose your old clothes. (You'll save money, keep those old favorites, and help a local entrepreneur!) When you are valuing your money and the things that you can buy with it, you are valuing all the hard work you have done to earn that money. And you are valuing yourself.

➤ Take the time to really think about the items that you buy. Is that sweater truly your best color? If not, don't settle for less than what will make you look great! Does your best friend really need that silly just-for-fun gift? Maybe they would appreciate a phone call more.

➤ Take care of your home which is, after all, an extension of yourself. It's also probably the biggest expense you have. You work very hard to pay for it so take care of it so it can take care of you. Put money into home improvement when you can. Get solar energy. Or wind, hydro, biomass, or whatever else you can manage. Not only will this help save the environment, you will also be taking away dollars from big corporations many of whom are entwined with Middle Eastern regimes that definitely don't support a Value Economy. Solar energy will also provide a much better source of energy if the power lines go down. And again, you are taking money away from big corporations and distributing it to the masses, i.e. you. (If you rent, there are a surprising number of ways to either get solar on your building or at least make sure that you are paying for electricity that is generated by the wind, water, or sun.)

Valuing Ourselves: Educate

➤ "Learn something new every day," goes the old saying and these days it is absolutely essential in the business environment. Businesses are investing millions of dollars in employee training as new technologies seem to appear faster and faster each year. We have to be constantly learning just to keep up! Take full advantage of the training your company has to offer.

➤ There has been an explosion of education opportunities in the last couple of decades with the advent of the internet. Courses from well-known universities are being opened to hundreds of thousands of students (so-called MOOCs—Massive Open Online Courses), sometimes even for free. If you've always wanted to go back to school for a second degree, there has never been a better time in human history.

➤ We humans are curious creatures. We like to learn especially when we can do it at our own pace. So follow your curiosity and watch documentaries on the latest science innovations, go see a local production of Shakespeare, or pick up that guitar you haven't touched since college. Get curious!

➤ Although there are more online opportunities than ever before, there is still a massive need for teachers, courses, and even buildings as schools, colleges, and universities are stretching to meet the demands and needs of students all over the world. Developing countries seem to be building a new college every day. In the U.S., sometimes students can't get the courses they need to finish their degrees. We need to keep working to improve our education system, training our future teachers and professors, and providing them with the fair pay, materials, and facilities that they need to do their job well.

➤ We are facing more complex and serious challenges to our survival as a species than ever before. We really do need all hands on deck. We need more teachers teaching all ages and abilities, we need more scientists researching climate change, cures for diseases, ways to produce more food for a growing population, and we need more engineers to build cities in new ways we can't yet imagine. And we need more astronauts. Really. We're going to go to Mars one of these days. And Venus. And back to the Moon. And probably a whole lot of other places. We're going to because we can and it'll be fun. But first, we need to get studying!

Valuing Each Other: Encourage

➤ There's a whole lot of stress in the world today. A few kind words from a friend or even a stranger can make a big difference.

➤ One of the toughest issues we are dealing with today is the impossible physical standards we are holding our young people to, especially our girls. Rates of weight imbalance—both over- and under-weight kids—have never been so high. Many, many people are trying to do something about the problem with mixed results. Some of the solutions just seem to make the problem worse. But we have to keep trying. The best thing we can do at this point is to stop focusing on superficial standards of outer beauty and keep working to help young people understand that true beauty really does come from inside. Actually, we need to do this with older people as well. I recently was shocked to hear a good-looking middle-aged successful professional woman I've known for many years say that she felt her love life was over as she was now over the hill! Just as the success of the Value Economy depends on us valuing our creativity over cash, valuing your own unique beauty over the latest ridiculous advertising-generating fashion ideal is essential to creating a world we all want to live in.

➤ A few groups of people in our society don't get nearly enough acknowledgement and encouragement so I'm singling them out here for special mention.

➤ Law enforcement. If you're in law enforcement, thank-you. Now, before you brush that off, take that in for a moment. I know—it's hard—you're not used to being acknowledged. A lot of the work you do is in the shadows and dealing with people who don't appreciate what you do. (This may be an understatement.) So, pause, take a deep breath and just let that acknowledgement in. And then ask for a raise! If you're not in law enforcement, take a moment and realize how safe you are. Or just turn on the news and watch what's going on in the news. There are men and women out there dealing with crime who are 100% committed to your safety and security. Think about that for a moment and then thank them the next chance you have. Police officers in particular are having a tough time right now. There's a whole lot of anti-police sentiment out there. Some of it is justified but a lot is not. Most of these men and women are doing a very tough job and handling it pretty well. They deserve our full support. And instead of complaining about how bad a few officers are, what about finding other ways to support the law enforcement in your community to make it better? Or, if you really have a problem with the way law enforcement is happening in your community, then you may not know this but you have just volunteered yourself to fix it. Constructively. By engaging in dialogue. Listening. And maybe even signing up to help them do their job. And give them that raise.

➤ The Military—If you're in the military or have served, thank-you. Similarly to law enforcement officers, military personnel also deal with the dark side of humanity but this time, it's at a global level. Much of what our men and women in uniform take on is, by nature, confrontational but they also do a lot of humanitarian work for which they don't get nearly enough credit. In both ways, however, thousands of our armed services personnel do their job with humility, courage, and to the best of their ability every day under circumstances and conditions that can best be described as "challenging" on an easy day. Acknowledge them. They also need a raise. We could be doing a much better job taking better care of both our active duty personnel and our vets. We're getting there slowly but making sure that vets are valued and included in our communities is essential to creating a Value Economy.

➤ Teachers - If you are a teacher you already know how tough a job it is. Thank-you for taking it on. (If you aren't but you're a parent, you probably have an inkling.) Though they often say how much they love their jobs, and we often say how wonderful our teachers are, we certainly aren't showing them this. They are some of the best educated people and least well-paid in our country. So, let's pay them. Pay them and see how many more young people want to join this profession. Pay them and see how kids respond. Pay them and see just how far we can advance in research and culture and all these wonderful human arts and sciences. Let's just do it.

➤ Healthcare professionals. If you work in health care, you already know how broken the system is. A lot of the people I talk to who are involved in it are hopeful that things are going to get better. Meanwhile, they figure out ways to work around it. Pharmacists think outside the box and recommend cheaper generic drugs when they can. Or they get coupons for their patients. Doctors give patients the loads of free samples they get in their offices to ease the financial burden. Many hospitals now have advocates to help patients and their families navigate the byzantine healthcare marketplace. And of course, there are thousands of online forums where people compare notes, offer advice, and support each other. But it's not enough and it's not as simple as Obamacare vs. No Obamacare. Let's face it—the system has been broken for a while, and the new Affordable Healthcare Act is far from perfect. We need to keep up the pressure on our lawmakers to fix this.

Valuing Each Other:
Pay Fairly

➤ Tip 20%. Even when I've received poor service I've tipped 20% and sometimes even more. Why? Because waiters are among the least well paid people in our society. They work very hard in frequently stressful workplaces dealing with very difficult people for very little pay. What we pay for their labor does not reflect reality. I know how hard these people who are usually just barely getting by work. I waitressed briefly when I was young (I am a terrible waitress by the way.) and have understood from that moment how utterly wrong the pay scale is for restaurant workers. The move toward higher minimum wages in many states is a step in the right direction but not nearly enough. So, tip people. It's an opportunity to give people at the very low end of the wage scale a big boost. (Yes, I know the companies should be paying them more. But they're not.)

➤ Tip anyway. Some hotels now frown on this but again, it's another way to level the playing field for people at the bottom of the food chain. And again, you are making a huge difference in these people's lives.

➤ When you tip people generously, you are valuing them more. And when you value others more, you will find that you also value yourself more.

➤ Pay more when you can. If you are at a restaurant and you get fantastic service, tip more than 20%. And tell their manager.

➤ Pay your employees fairly. And make absolutely 100% sure you are paying your female and minority employees equally to your white male employees. Even if you think you are, double-check to be sure. It's amazing how prejudices can creep in even when you think you're being completely unbiased. Take the time to make sure you're paying fairly.

➤ If you own a small business and really are paying your employees as much as you can but know they probably need more, work with them so that they can hold that second job, or take classes to improve their job prospects. Find ways to help them make ends meet. Maybe that working parent really could bring their preschooler in for a few hours after daycare ends? Your employees will appreciate your efforts and it will show up in the quality of their work.

➤ Promote education. Our modern workplaces are changing so quickly that constant training is now a necessity. Be sure your employees are up to speed. If they're not, help them get there. And even if it doesn't seem directly work-related, working with your employees to further their personal education goals may help you in unexpected ways. Plus, you'll have happier employees.

➤ You don't always need to bargain. Sometimes we can bargain too much. If your bargaining skills are getting in the way of treating someone you do business with fairly, then you may not be getting the deal you think you are. If that person isn't as skilled at bargaining as you are, they may feel that, having not gotten the fair end of the deal, that they also don't have an obligation to do their best work. Sometimes bargaining hard is not a good idea.

➤ Pay for quality. If you have fallen in love with a piece of art, pay for it. Pay the artisan who put their blood, sweat, and tears into a piece what they truly deserve not what you can beat them down to. And pay for music, movies, and other forms of art available for free but illegally online. This is the way to thank artists for the beautiful things they have brought into your life.

➤ If you hire someone to do a job whether it's babysitting, cleaning your house, gardening, fixing something in your home, pay them fairly. You will get better service. You will feel better. And you will be doing more for the economy than you realize. You're taking a stand that everyone deserves fair pay.

➤ Stop using and supporting the use of slave labor by buying cheaply made foreign clothing and non-fair trade goods.

➤ Support fair wages for those who work at the bottom of the jobs market—maids, farm workers, construction workers, temp workers, etc . . . Paying these people living wages not only helps them but will help all of us in lowering the social service bills we all contribute to via our taxes.

➤ Pay your taxes to fight corruption, crime and terrorism. Most of us can't do much in the battle against crime and terrorism but we can support those who do. We need to pay our judiciary, law enforcement, and military enough to do their jobs. We don't need to waste money on government projects that our law enforcement and military say they don't need. We do need to make sure they have everything they tell us that they do need to do their jobs effectively.

➤ In recent years, the idea of a "universal basic income" has been gaining steam. This theory involves setting a minimum income level for all the citizens of a country so that everyone would have enough money to pay for housing, food, and other basic necessities. It could also eliminate and/or streamline welfare programs. Although I appreciate the generous spirit of the people behind this idea, I also believe that people still have a basic desire and need to feel useful to society. We should continue to encourage all human beings to find work that is meaningful and that allows them to express their creativity to the fullest whether or not there is a basic income or some other system in place.

Valuing Each Other: Share

➤ Besides Airbnb and Uber, there are tons of other ways to share (and save money). Clothing, power tools, kitchenware, you can find a way to share just about everything these days. But remember, play fair too. Don't overcharge for those things you share, and don't under- or overpay.

➤ Share your bills. If you are in an apartment building, consider banding together with your fellow renters and paying for one internet connection. You can use boosters throughout the building and you could lower your bill quite a lot.

➤ Trade services or goods. A close friend and I have done this so many times over the years I've lost track. Usually, I need some item of clothing repaired and she needs some editing or proof-reading. It's a win-win for both of us. A couple of times, we have even turned it into a win-win-win when I paid for her services but the payment went to her favorite charity. We love making these kinds of trades.

➤ Share yourself. With fewer and fewer jobs out there, finding meaningful work is going to get a lot harder. That's where our creativity really needs to kick in. Have a friend who's an artist? How about starting an art gallery with them? Or maybe open a pottery studio to teach new students? Maybe even teach yourself something by helping new refugees learn English while you learn about their culture? There are millions of possibilities.

➤ One sure sign that you might need to consider sharing yourself more is if you have a business or are in charge of a department at a company and are concerned about who can back you up if you have to go on sick leave or you are considering retirement. Training a replacement may seem counterintuitive to holding on to your position but in reality, it's smart business to create a back-up.

➤ And if you are one of the millions of craftspeople out there who do such beautiful work, please consider sharing your art with younger people who are interested. There's more of a need for great artisans and craftspeople than you might realize. One micro-sized niche I've heard of recently is for a glass-blower trained in the sciences who can create specialized beakers for a tech university's experiments. There are definitely not that many openings for that particular career but it certainly is essential to the development of our science knowledge.

Valuing Community: Participate

➤ Reach out to your community. Check on your neighbors and not just after a natural disaster. Know who they are. You can be there for them and they may be there for you when you most need it.

➤ Get involved in local events. Get a library card. Find out about local history through the Historical Society. Be a part of local fundraising efforts. Run or walk a 10k.

➤ Grow vegetables, herbs, fruits, flowers. You're not going to be self-sufficient but a garden will provide you with (a) exercise, (b) fun, and (c) something to share with friends, family, and neighbors. And go to your local farmer's market and check out what everyone else is up to.

➤ Make things. Create something that you can share with friends and neighbors. Or maybe just give away as gifts for holidays and other celebrations. Try canning or freezing fresh vegetables or fruits even if you have to buy them at a local farmer's market. Or maybe try your hand at making a unique piece of furniture, something not from a well-known Swedish retailer. Or try knitting a sweater, maybe a scarf if you've never knitted anything before. Do something with your hands. And find others who do as well. And then you may find yourself showing others something you've made and teaching them how you did it!

➤ Volunteer. Is there something in your community you're complaining about? Guess what? You've just volunteered yourself to fix it! Don't like the appearance of your downtown? That's right—you're on the clean-up crew now. Better yet, create an "enterprise zone" to support local businesses and draw in customers. Concerned about crime? Start a neighborhood watch program. Concerned about obesity in young people? Organize a fundraising walk and find a sponsor.

➤ Most of us in America live in cities and the suburbs and the rest of the world is following this trend. It's easy when you live in a fairly modern city or a better-off community near a city to think that there's not a lot of poverty around. But you'd be wrong to think that. In rural areas, the poor are often hidden far off the main highways in towns that are falling apart. Many of these area are also ridden with drugs. In the outskirts or in enclaves of big cities where the main roads don't go, you can also find pockets of desperately poor people not unlike what we used to consider "Third World." It's hard to face this but it is absolutely necessary that we do so. We need to reach out to these people with compassion but also dignity. If we don't address the poverty we aren't seeing in the developed world, how can we hope to address it globally? So, please, reach out when you can. Include everyone in your community.

Valuing Community: Invest Local

➤ Shop local. In a world where people are paid almost nothing (and truly nothing when they are held as slaves) to make cheap goods sold by big companies in affluent Western countries, we need to support our local shopkeepers and craftspeople. Yes, I know the prices are better in the big box stores and online, and it's more convenient. It's also literally killing people—both abroad in poorly regulated factories and here when people lose their jobs. There are a lot of movements to promote local businesses including "Small Business Saturday" (which comes after Black Friday). And if you do need to buy something non-local, try to buy it with a Fair Trade label. (Fair Trade coffee and chocolate are excellent ways to do this. . . .)

➤ Start a social enterprise. Find a way to help those in your community who might need a boost by coming up with a way to start a business that gives back. If you need ideas, one way of generating them is to start a Soup Dinner. Tell people in your community that you are hosting an event—everyone brings a few dollars and a simple food dish. Then you invite people to share ideas for a social enterprise. Everyone votes on the best idea and that person takes the cash pooled for the evening. (This idea has actually gone global. For more info, check out the Detroit Soup project's website at detroitsoup.com.)

➤ Invest local. These places—where our families, friends, school mates, favorite coffee shops and restaurants are, where our bookshops and farmer's markets are set-up, where we go to work out our bodies, hang out to play a game or two with our best friends, and meet in places of worship for our souls, these are the places we need to build, invest in, and participate in fully.

Valuing Community: Invest Global

➤ Connect your community to other communities across the world. You're probably already connected in numerous ways and don't even realize it. The best way to do this is just to start talking to people. What you find out may surprise you.

➤ Give globally. In a way, when you give to charities that are helping people in the developing world, you are investing in the future of humanity. We're all in this together. As much as some would like to believe, our countries and societies are irrevocably intertwined at this point and the only way we are going to survive is if we all work together. That means everyone. All 7 billion and counting of us.

There are probably about a million other tips you can think of to help bring about a Value Economy. I've left plenty of extra space in this book for you to add your own notes and ideas. If you'd like to share them with others on the website at *www.TheValueEconomy.com*, please feel free.

Creating this Book

The idea of The Value Economy was born out of my own frustration and exasperation with the "non-recognition" of my first novel, a labor of love which took fourteen years of my life to complete.

In the process of writing The Value Economy, I discovered that at least part of what I was doing was creating my own path forward from that place of not feeling valued to being at peace with my art and ways of self-expression.

As I wrote, I also began following my own suggestions. Redoing my resume, researching and learning about other paths I might pursue, encouraging friends and others I spoke to about this book in their own pursuits, remembering even when I didn't have much cash to still be generous, and realizing I needed to be far more involved in my many communities.

A friend who was the first person to read this book also found herself doing something similar.

I may create a workbook for this. I may not. I'm not sure yet. I also like the fact that the book is less rigid and allows for you to create your own very unique path forward as you Value Yourself, Your Friends and Family, and Your Community. Good luck.

About the Author

Heather McConnell fell in love with writing, reading, books and words when she was ten years old. She has worked as a newspaper journalist, book editor, temporary office worker in advertising and P.R. firms, bookstore manager in six different retail chains, and online medical e-newsletter/website production wrangler but has always written in her spare hours—letters, diaries, journals, stories, essays, and thoughts about the world. In June of 2015, she published her first novel, An Invisible Woman in Afghanistan. She is hard at work on her second novel, An Invisible Woman in Tamil Nadu. She lives near the New England seacoast.

Endnotes

[1] Sugata Mitra, "Kids can teach themselves," TED talk, http://www.ted.com/talks/sugata_mitra_shows_how_kids_teach_themselves.

[2] Michael Goldfarb, "US election 2016: The 40-year hurt," BBC News, March 26, 2016, http://www.bbc.com/news/magazine-35890784.

[3] Curtin SC, Warner M, Hedegaard H. Suicide rates for females and males by race and ethnicity: United States, 1999 and 2014. NCHS Health E-Stat. National Center for Health Statistics. April 2016. http://www.cdc.gov/nchs/data/hestat/suicide/rates_1999_2014.htm.

[4] U.S. Dept. of Labor, Bureau of Labor Statistics, Economic News Release, June 24, 2016, American Time Use Survey Summary, http://www.bls.gov/news.release/atus.nr0.htm.

[5] World Health Organization, Joint WHO/UNICEF/World Bank News Release, Child mortality rates plunge by more than half since 1990 but global MDG target missed by wide margin, Sept. 9, 2015, http://www.who.int/mediacentre/news/releases/2015/child-mortality-report.

[6] MDGMonitor, Achieve Universal Primary Education (UN Millennium Development Goal #2), http://www.mdgmonitor.org/mdg-2-achieve-universal-primary-education.

[7] Joshua S. Goldstein and Steven Pinker, "The decline of war and violence," *The Boston Globe*, April 15, 2016 (http://www.bostonglobe.com/opinion/2016/04/15/the-decline-war-and-violence/lxhtEplvppt0Bz9kPphzkL/story.html).

www.ingramcontent.com/pod-product-compliance
Lightning Source LLC
Chambersburg PA
CBHW071838200526
45169CB00020B/1770